This book is dedicated
to the family I was born into,
the family my wife and I raised,
and to all families in between.

CLOSE TO HOME
haiku and other poems

Copyright 2013 by David E. LeCount

All rights reserved. No part of this book may be reproduced or utilized in any form or by any means, electronic or mechanical, including photocopying, recording, or by any information storage and retrieval system, without permission in writing from the publisher.

Day'sEye Press and Studios
PO Box 628
El Granada, CA 94018
info@dayseyepressandstudios.com
www.dayseyepressandstudios.com

ISBN: 978-0-9619714-4-1
Printed in the United States of America

Cover photos by the author
Cover and text design copyright 2013
by Diane Lee Moomey

Author's Note

In one stone or turtle shell, one feels a passion to live forever and a recognition that it cannot happen. In the leaning of a favorite willow tree is the love of beauty and ugliness that cannot be separated, and that cannot be owned. So it is that what we love and hate is terminal and eternal. Out of all poetry comes the longing for what we can never have, and never lose. The holding on and the letting go.

The poems that follow attempt to capture places and people who were, and could have been, with a passion for the paradox that holds life together. I have made no attempt to make them into typical haiku nor an attempt to keep them from it. While I was in China, the La Honda ones grew; while I was in La Honda the China poems grew.

It was in this way the places grew into each other as times did. It was in this way both were Close To Home.

CLOSE TO HOME
haiku and other poems

by David E. LeCount

DAY'S EYE PRESS AND STUDIOS
EL GRANADA, CALIFORNIA

the poems

Close to Home

Housewrecking —
the nail-puller shrieks
into the autumn air

                    Open the wind,
                    let the bee out!
                    just smell those lilacs!

Following its loneliness
down the trail, the solo quail
slowly fills its craw

swaying hammock —
the wind just got up
and left

                        throwing lettuce
                to the geese — one eats
                   from another's wing

within these barnacles —
the hiss of a tide,
its seeping voice

        finished,
he drags the broom behind him:
      a trail without footsteps

in the bread line
a mother nurses from one breast
then the other

        striking the match
     on the gritty old brick
       my finger lights up

after it pees on her hand
grandma sets the toad gently
in the rose bed

apricot warmth —
on my tongue one taste
of the summer sun

her dark eyes searching
the heart of the storm —
rain beads on lashes

rainy stairs —
as I climb them a tree frog
hops on my shoe

                              convertible at the lake
                                      all stars
                                pour into the car

how to open the jam jar?
only greasy fingers
this early, this morning!

rocky shoreline —
the chilled loon calls
to its echo

                before crossing the paper's edge
                          the young spider
                        checks its footing

reaching for the wind:
out of the car the child's arm,
a flapping sleeve

            toad wallow …
                 eyes only
            above the leaves

strong silence of stone —
a pika shrieks the warning
of the hawk shadow

                hidden corner —
          a mousetrap goes off
          by the weight of dust

> throwing horseshoes,
> I claim "interference"
> on a fluttering butterfly

"Road Under Construction":
signs end where
the real bumps begin

> morning, low tide —
> a starfish in the pool
> dozes in the sun

blue sage —
a path of deer prints
light as shadows

late summer —
fallen apples roll by themselves
into the corral

collecting firewood —
already, wet undersides
half way to earth smell

Close to Home

winter arcade —
gum wrappers and cigarette butts
sink in the rain

                                      boiling crawdad —
                                          tide smell swelling
                                                into the kitchen

the swan pillows
its beak under a back wing,
paddling forward

beach campfire —
driftwood smoke smells
of sea not pine

a skiff to their village —
the Aleuts don't talk
but watch our footsteps[1]

country outhouse . . .
down the stone path
a rattler goes

desert railroad crossing —
a mouse darts across
without waiting

on the riverbank
the snake admires itself
full length in the sun

goat milking —
late at night the rats
stand by and watch

fencing in mosquitoes
with the tent netting
seems to work

              by the stream side
              I first taste the cold,
                  then the water

seal head riding
wave crests — the white
that flows from it

in the dry moonlight
the web reveals
bright patches of dust

                              swan-loose lake —
              such grace of ripple and wake
                       in the autumn winds

the drifting goose
walks onto the bank as if
stepping from a shower

stomach growling
in the empty church ... still desires
to be hidden

in doing laundry
I find my clean old key,
but to what?

in the cactus shadow
a lizard turns its tail
towards the setting sun

driving in silence,
I make up songs to accompany
windshield wiper blades

in pitiful sleep
the dog chases a nightmare
into the rug

tonight, old memories
return faster than old friends —
full autumn moon

the orb weaver
repairs her web, knitting
with her rear end

                      shaking fingers —
            the old fisherman steadies
                a hook with the worm

the yellow dogwood
leans against the window,
a self-made bouquet

Close to Home

the old temple bell —
a silver track of the snail
rings in silence

                                                  a goose warns
                                                    of trespassers
                                                who are quail!

ghost town —
hear the buckboards and stagecoaches
come and go

hazy moon
a grasshopper jumps
out of the fog

a shadow
in the closet at night —
is my coat hanging itself?

Pounding breakers, long after
my burning head hits the pillow,
tumble and resound again

          they discuss news:
      her hearing-aid on high,
              his on low

in falling winds,
the butterfly rises
in circles

           only in the rain,
              the frog hops
        to miss the puddles

morning loneliness —
I invent words the quail
might be saying

                                        a logger's suspenders —
                                        he walks towards the beer
                                                with sawdust eyelids

haunting wilderness:
come inside my silence
and never go!

Grasses rolling into grasses —
the wind burnishes the tops
of all that's green

                                  in my jeans pocket
                    the lint that fills fingernails,
                                      but not a dime

ocean wind chimes —
the salt rust tone
deepens the breakers

Mexican jumping bean:
  warmer in his pocket
as he crosses the border

under the umbrella
the moth with the limp wings
waits too!

Snail out of your shell —
    at first no horns
  then the coast is clear

ladle-stirred leaves
from the well bottom
black with age

moonlit pond —
koi explode
into the falling star

the street-sweeper stops,
spits his morning tobacco
into the gutter

my old jeans —
I'd wash them but for their smell
of mountain sage

                    halted in the air,
          the hummingbird's straw:
                      a beak of nectar

behind the gauze,
the berry pickers lift
morning fog

twilight swallows
sail quickly into the dusk
for one last bite

                        facing the North wind,
                    I slump lower and lower
                    without finding warmth

in a grooming frenzy
the youngest gosling
unties my shoelace

    a dictionary for words
        she says in her sleep:
            that's what I need

shoreline canoe — abandoned
but for the tadpoles hatching
within the warm bilge

            So small a defect
        that I need my glasses
            to fix my glasses

Close to Home

        raft on the lake —
the smell of stale rubber
        inflated by breath

grizzly fishing —
with one great paw the salmon tail
swipes the air

        dry field of deer horns
peering above the grass
        after each mouthful

swelling breakers —
the young seal swept to the sand
can't swim back

                                            a stray cat
                              arrives at my doorstep
                                  only to share its fleas

in the sand box —
ants frenzied
by a popsicle stick

down Sears Ranch Road[2] —
he spins his wheelchair,
loving summer dust

                              rural outhouse —
                    some flies off duty,
                            some busy

rain shelter —
one old man appraises
another's umbrella

a frog too
in this sudden rain
crosses by bridge

sculpting dams of leaves:
boys repair and unrepair
the rain's path

lingerie drawer —
the daddy-long-legs
mingles with lace

                    the crawdad's path:
                         half crawl
                         half swim

dawn hayloft —
returning bats
make their silence felt

                           on the suds
                of the great waterfall rides
                      a belly-up gnat

autumn woodlands —
the doe licks mosquitoes
off her nose

                              desolate stones —
              the howling and wind and
                                  I love them

after my bath
the fleas climb back on
the stubble of my legs

a hot stone
the fallen young leaf
wilts alone

                          A curious calf —
                            her ears perk up
                            sniffing a thistle

along the seashore,
pampas grass blooms sideways
in the wake of a white wind

Monday morning —
she still lies dreaming
of a pastry shop

autumn fly —
first he wants indoors,
then outdoors

Is it the sunset
or the persimmon that peeks
last thru the dusk?

Close to Home

        where we gardened,
      now even thistles wither
    from the slow fury of frost

no one knows Buddha
but this snail in the rain
brakes down his nose

          hummingbird wings
              gone
          before their blur

on my knees
I welcome the New Year
looking for my glasses

                    morning bus —
          the smell of overnight gum
              and stale cigarettes.
     how fresh-sounding the rain
     as the door shuts behind me

leftover autumn apples —
to dine on in frost
this coyote morning

forgetting the Latin name:
the taste left over
is 'sour grass'

                                        bitter cold —
                                  a finchless limb
                            and chickadee silence

beyond the bend,
the road is ice
darker than itself

bamboo flute:
the lingering ache and echo
of autumn wind

carving a walking-stick—
the young boys's cane
topped with mermaid's breasts

the tide sweeps ashore
with sand and battered shells
this endless moon

threading the needle
closest to the one squinting eye
that works best

mountain summit —
words into the wind whispered
quiet and cold

alone, the frog
can't quite swallow the fly
without one more gulp

an old bra thrown out —
but not before one more twirl
of girlish delight

                                      old fingers —
                       dialing the phone,
                they poke like a witch's

in the swirling scum
a willow leaf cannot
exit the current

rug cleaning —
she swears at the toys
she gave for Christmas

San Francisco Zoo
"monkey island" —
I root for the sleeping ones
who disdain peanuts

in the moonlight,
an unblown dandelion
brightens the autumn sky

in the car mirror,
her lipstick turning
the wrong color

antlers in the brush
hold still:
the silence deafens

wind chimes
the hummingbird can't drink from
have left a song

Close to Home

        in the deep pool
        a leaf moves aside
        to let the crawdad pass

lost in thought,
the priest hangs up his collar
on an absent peg

        from the dryer—
        a household cocoon
        the touch of lint

her swelling breasts
the tightening shirt:
these autumn winds

a sun-dial
in the morning fog
drips into dew

stepping off
the merry-go-round:
the earth's spin

to pour tea:
do you watch the spout
or the cup?

                        its ways unknown
              the hummingbird's tasting
                          defies the sky

her winter sweater:
it's the holes at the elbows
that charm me

this autumn —
the tire swing dangles
only a rope

through barbed wire
the butterfly flits
taking my breath away

a water lily:
dragonflies land here
to mate cautiously

        feeding the starlings —
a woman with her sleeping bag
            in a shopping cart

a caterpillar's gait:
each foot rides the ripple
up and down

           towering gnats:
       rising on sunlight
      circle their circles

sacred dusk,
where the bells come from
a goat's collar

                                          old Bible —
                    a moth that was reading Job
                                          died there

old sofa —
the shapes where we sat
ready for sale

Close to Home

in her purse,
lipstick has slid to the bottom —
her civil cursing

                            saluting the flag,
                    the old Veterans pass by
                      more boylike than boys

my father,
your strained steps
and tottering balance —
this summer's end

                    lint in the pocket,
              and an old theatre ticket
                    the jacket emerges

the giraffe grazes
where the zoo has given it
grass aloft!

                         the boy's fort
                   in the tall grasses
                cannot hide all sneezes

her son off to college —
she weeps
at the full moon

old sisters
don't talk of husbands,
just new teacups

sweeping the walk
the reddest maple leaf rises
to top the pile

a pop-up
at the country ballyard
baffles the swallows

                        pumping up a tire —
              the bicycle noises attract
                          the dog's nose

the frog
in silent prayer
clears its throat

Close to Home

learning to shoot?
the child cannot both hold his breath
and squeeze

                                              dank cave —
                            the Girl Scouts gossip
                                about what bats do

stuttering salesman at the door —
no one dares to
finish his sentences

our baby-sitter's smile
when we say "next time"—
too quickly gone

city playground —
half-dressed boys play at stoning
cherry blossoms

morning dewdrop,
pointed out by my finger,
bursts

Close to Home

        at the country dump
    seagulls rising and falling
          on summer's smells

in the lightning
a crane swallowing its fish
all beak

         in the fast lane,
    the laden-down glass truck
            passing

cleaning the stall
her pigtails sway
as she bends in her jeans

                her shade of lipstick
         in this lonely country town
                   a stranger too

off to college —
the oldest son forgets
to take his pillow

Close to Home

fly season —
a country woman stitching
the screen door

                                        zoo moat —
                     a fly on cotton candy
                 having walked zebra dung

around the corner
the cat scrapes her fur
on angles

the old calligrapher —
     each hand paints
     a different poem

combing her hair slowly —
I feel the autumn winds
at my back

            the smudge pots
        below the orange trees
            grow ghost shapes

Close to Home

                    weeds to pull —
          the goat's shaking beard
                chews sideways

I am the one who,
for the moonlight,
sweeps the stone walk

                  his leg in a cast —
          the urgency to scratch,
        a poker just out of reach

lizard fence —
not a railing
that doesn't crawl

                              beloved slippers —
                                deep tooth marks
                                of three dogs ago

hiking up her skirt
she straddles the berry patch
in sandals!

on the barbed wire
coyote pelts warn others
through the fog[3]

                        hippie's pigtail —
                  she's braided her gray
                with bachelor buttons

in a mowed field
the stone leaves a tuft
that can't be baled

chasing grasshoppers —
a boy's hands right there
just after they've gone

a silence
in the rose
reddens the dusk

busybody geese —
the coming and goings
of the manure-spreader

                              firefly light
                              turns on
                              this dark

a candle drips
in dim light — wine
pours over the thumb

                    down the smile of Buddha,
                         bird droppings
                         whiten the rain

laundry room —
she steps on a cockroach
during the spin cycle!

                              cleaning the stable —
                              a summer mushroom
                              small and sickly

the bats flee
out of the bells —
Sunday morning

from her purse,
nothing comes or goes without
her look of bewilderment

                              a "lost" puppy —
                    no one will miss him
                          my son argues

summer merry-go-round,
holding on tightly —
mother's merciless fun

in the wind —
the hopscotch token
takes three jumps

China: The Journey

customs and baggage —
the one with a machine gun
checks my stubs

                    the bamboo scaffold
              fifteen stories high: a man
                weaves one knot at dusk

balancing bricks:
his woven basket poles
rock his shoulders!

                    two Buddhist nuns,
                their robes flying, rush
            into Hong Kong's McDonald's

Beijing darkness ...
a mule and a man's belongings
clomp past

                          the new honking
                     of a sea of bicycles —
                      Beijing willow road

shaving off the thorns
with a pocket knife —
poor rose seller

Close to Home

Confucius-faced man
walking into my eyes —
the centuries!

                    ancient eyes —
        the patience of one's waiting
                reflected on waters

the Great Wall —
climbing with me I feel
the breathing hordes

everyone honking —
a goose in a cage rides
on the bicycle seat

foot of the Great Wall —
a young girl shows me
her pet cicadas

Guilin
Reed Flute Cave

empty cormorant basket —
what sadness!
what happiness![4]

        in the cave shadows:
the cormorants wait, grooming,
            for passing fish

bow of the boat —
one Mandarin and one Cantonese talk
writing on their palms

Li River —
three thousand years flow
past the water buffalo

water buffalo
at dusk —
a pool full of noses

Li River boat . . .
I steer scenery for a moment
as the captain smokes

                        Reed Flute Cave —
              with the power out, bats
            cling to wet stone smells

beggar children —
the toys they sell dirtied
from being slept with

Tokyo

typhoon season —
the roof of the night train
sways as it pours

thunder?
the train overhead speeds
faces into blurs

typhoon season —
swans in a Tokyo pond
groom each others necks

Close to Home

        the dripping temple —
        puddles that would suit
          one stone and a frog

in the subway
she waits for any old seat —
eyebrows fresh with rain

        lunching with the monks —
        one pushes the odd-tasting fish
          to the side of the plate

beat the drum!
The visitor who is coming
may be Buddha

                      the bald monks at lunch —
                            how funny,
                       my beard and curly hair!

Close to Home

The Silk Road

Xi'an[5] peasant:
he laughs at his tongue
spoken from my mouth

                    old mule cart thumping
              past the ringing bicycles —
                        echoing stars

the Forbidden City —
a peasant traces a thousand years
in the sandalwood

Beijing

        old friend, the Great Wall
            and new graffiti
          where hordes are silent

eerie midnight welding —
past the lane of willows
a duck, a bicycle

              down narrow alleys
               in a rented car, for
an uncertain address — Peking dusk

Tian Shan[6]

>my eyes close,
>and the young camel's, too,
>down the Silk Road

the yurt, the Kazakh,
the bowl: all here but this stranger,
a bearded one, a souvenir

>burro taxis
>wait at the street market —
>branches near for eating

asleep on the bank —
a swallow flies up his shorts —
the driver's laughter

                                atop the minaret
                      the swallow brings mud
                                    for its design

across passes —
the face of Flaming Mountain
ripples with heat

Thousand Buddha Caves —
infidels who painted mud
over Uighur Buddha's eyes

                        mountain-sized dune —
            the wind sharpens its edges
                            with a whistle

driving through the Gobi
I beep at the Tian Shan
to hear my smallness

horseback —
high in the Tian Shan
I loosen an eagle

fallen asleep
on a slab of rock —
mountain of Heavens

desert train view:
the face of each rock
ripples with heat

Close to Home

        old carpet factory —
        hands that fly at knots
        into colors

Gobi Desert —
the aching clack of the train
on the hot tracks echoes

        the staring faces
        from an adobe window —
        a tourist's beard

Han Great Wall —
a wind sweeps clean
the two last gates

a city of drivers,
all mad with horns — donkeys
fleeing the quirts

drifting to sleep,
I still rock to the echo
of the wet train tracks

Close to Home

camel hump
rising before me into the dune —
a crescent moon

                              dusk oasis —
                       the camels link
            their lengthening shadows

Ten Thousand Buddhas
with faces of mud —
unreached lotus ceiling

familiar oasis —
the camels sucking water
nonstop

driving home on his bicycle
with butane tank
and pink-dressed daughter

hospital of Dunhuang[7] —
doctors, masks down, smiling,
gather around our pictures from home

Close to Home

        piglets lost on the street
        grunting between bicycles —
            that mad balancing!

sweltering heat —
two swans idling under willows
trailing reflections

        brick fences topped
        with broken bottles —
        the peasant's "Keep out!"

swallows' nests
on the Wild Goose Pagoda . . .
a clear full moon

                           unbroken sounds
                  of the aching cicadas —
                              sweltering heat

seen through dreams —
the one where I sit at home,
three sons speaking at once

Close to Home

down ancient streets:
morning horse and rooster sounds
rise in the sun

                                      jade factory —
                     polished eyes in shapes
                           of fleeing fish

country hospital —
small bare feet pace
the mud brick floor

old men on their haunches
playing majiang by moonlight —
they move, shadows

Shanghai acrobatics —
the pig cart on a scenic route
in this heat!

cicadas aboard
the plane — in flight with us,
the noises of China

Hong Kong

sampan ride —
the toddler overboard!
and father's one jump!

city of neon stars —
that old longing here
for a clean desert sky

the stars tonight
draw the moths
to reflecting pools

a wake of perfume
as if nipples soft coolness
brushing quickly past

                homesick restlessness —
     an herbalist's shop, all snakes coiled
                    fangs on their tails

Close to Home

End Notes

1. This verse was inspired by a visit to an Aleut village. Most if not all native villagers in Alaska are suspicious of or timid with, outsiders. *(page 13)*

2. Sears Ranch Road is a steep road leading to La Honda Elementary School. *(page 32)*

3. Coyote pelts were hung on fence wires by ranchers to scare off living coyotes. *(page 64)*

4. In China, cormorants are used for fishing; an empty fish basket means sadness for the fisherman but happiness for the uncaught fish. *(page 74)*

5. Xi'an is the beginning of the ancient Silk Road. *(page 80)*

6. Tian Shan are the mountains in far western China separating it from Kazakhstan. *(page 82)*

7. Dunhuang is an ancient city along the Silk Road where an extraordinary collection of Buddhist art and manuscripts was discovered. *(page 89)*

www.ingramcontent.com/pod-product-compliance
Lightning Source LLC
Chambersburg PA
CBHW020920090426
42736CB00008B/728